Still Slaves in America

America

Working Together to Break the Chains of Poverty

Jocelyn Whitfield

ISBN: 1539839834
ISBN 13: 9781539839835

Table of Contents

Dedication

I dedicate this book to the millions of individuals, families, and children affected by generational poverty in America. Also, let me acknowledge the government programs that inspire people toward achieving the American Dream as well as the churches and congregations answering the call to care for the poor, to be their voices, and to advocate for them.

Acknowledgements

SPECIAL THANKS GO to my friend, colleague, and editor June Mickens, who has edited every page to make sure that my thoughts and words were congruent. I am also grateful to many of you who have inspired the writing of this book and encouraged me to place these words on paper. There are so many of you that I dare not mention one without mentioning others. Thank you.

Preface

*"It takes nothing to stay in poverty, but
everything to break free from it."*

Idowu Koyenikan

STILL SLAVES IN America is not a book for the faint of heart.
It is a book about poverty, those affected by it, and what we can do
together to ameliorate it in America's communities. The information shared is based on research, my experience working with groups
serving the poor and in local churches, and recent personal involve-
ment with homeless women and children. The book focuses on those
whom I have chosen to call "America's Modern-Day Slaves". They are
the women, men, and children chained to a system that enslaves
rather than empowers—a system designed by the government to
move them out of poverty but that instead has made them dependent on it. As a result, many today still live in poverty.

Poverty affects all of us. It is everyone's problem—the individual, family, church, government, and community. It impacts every

age, geographic location, religion, and race—whether white, black, or brown. Poverty cannot be hidden, and it does not discriminate. It shows up on America's streets and corners and in its cities and rural communities. It leaves behind boarded-up properties in inner-city neighborhoods and shanty houses in rural communities. Poverty walks the streets, sits on church steps, and sleeps on benches in front of government buildings and under bridges. The faces of poverty are people who are on welfare, disabled, addicted to drugs, suffering from mental health conditions, incarcerated, unemployed, and the working poor. In general, they are the faces of people who have fallen on hard times.

Because poverty affects all of us in some way, it will take all of us to provide realistic solutions to eradicate it. Together, we can establish a framework and pathway to self-sufficiency and economic independence for America's poor. Together, we can break the chains of poverty.

Still Slaves in America

Working Together to Break the Chains of Poverty

"Everyone has a right to peaceful coexistence, the basic personal freedoms, the alleviation of suffering, and the opportunity to lead a productive life...."

Jimmy Carter

Introduction

I AM WRITING this book because I am concerned about the future and destiny of the poor in America, and I am especially disheartened by what is happening in communities with people of African descent. I understand that poverty touches all ethnic and racial groups. However, in this discussion, I wish to have an open dialogue about my race—African Americans—and specifically about those living in the inner cities of America, who disproportionately live in poverty and who are dependent upon government systems to provide for their basic needs. Coupled with poverty, in most urban African-American neighbor-hoods, we see and hear about death, destruction, family turmoil, family separation, hopelessness, and psychological distress. We also find that what once was a people of so much hope, now is a people of broken spirit—a people who have lost direction and who experience great dysfunction. The World Health Foundation has labeled poverty as the world's "most ruthless killer" and "the greatest cause of suffering."

It wasn't always this way. I remember when it was quite different. As a young adult in the late 1960s, I remember what we looked like as a race. We were a strong, God-loving people—a tight-knit unit with an undying connection to family, an incredible work ethic, and pride in our skills, talents, and gifts. Despite discrimination, unusual cruelty, pain, and adversity, we still continued to be a viable force to be reck-oned with. In fact, we actually used adversity as a catalyst for working harder to achieve a better life for ourselves and our children. We were a village, raising up teachers, doctors, laborers, shipyard workers, law-yers, and people in many other professions. No job was beneath us if it would move us out of poverty. I remember African-American fathers and mothers working multiple jobs to ensure that their children were educated. I know this because my father was one of them.

But, today, for too many, it is different. In too many urban com-munities, we find an erosion of faith in God and a loss of self-respect, human dignity, purpose, and economic opportunity. Poverty has a way of devaluing human beings. It can become a catalyst for self-hatred. When people do not know who they are spiritually and are denied the opportunity to work and earn living wages, they lose self-worth and hope, and they begin down the path of self-hatred.

However, the truth is God doesn't discriminate. Our Creator has made all people equal and able to pursue a life of happiness and wellbe-ing. Our Founding Fathers embedded these truths in the Declaration of Independence by stating that, "We hold these truths to be self-evident, that all men are created equal, that they are endowed by their Creator with certain unalienable rights, that among these are Life, Liberty and the Pursuit of Happiness." What this means, in simpler terms, is that every human being is created by God, is to be equally treated, and is to have the chance for a good or flourishing life. These inalienable rights belong to each of us and are indisputable regardless of race or ethnic-ity. The right to those opportunities not only extends to people today but to generations to come. To deny this right is a grievous injustice.

Everyone comes into life wanting and seeking a good life, desiring an equal chance to rise on the ladder of wellbeing. Equality starts out as, and should remain, a staple in everyone's life. All people—regardless of race, socio-economic status, how we look, or where we come from—should have the right to human dignity and the chance to achieve great things in America. Yet, for too many, that is not so. When a people is denied the opportunity to work—to provide for themselves and their children—we will find a people who have lost hope in themselves, in God's ability to help them, and in the dream of a better future.

Embracing the subjects of poverty, equality, and slavery of any kind can be quite uncomfortable; it was for me. My discomfort had to take a back seat, however; this is a discussion that needed to be had. The intent of this book is not to denigrate either African Americans or the poor. My goal simply is to point to what I see as the sources of the poverty problem and to speak to what I believe keeps a people dependent upon a welfare system that, in its current form, will never allow them to prosper.

This may not be an easy book to read. You may find the issues and my discussion of them a bit controversial. I agree, and I will tell you that this was not an easy book to write. The first three chapters address what I consider to be modern-day slavery and briefly describe the people who are affected. The remaining chapters focus on government programs; the church's call to care for the poor; and the responsibility of the community, the individual, and the family.

The topic of poverty is multifaceted. It impacts both the human and the spiritual condition. When you read this book, I hope you will go beyond the social and historical ideas presented here and allow yourself to be awakened to the truth—human and spiritual. Then, you will know that the future of the poor is not as bleak as it may seem. There still is hope and faith—that every human being, desiring to work, can have the opportunity to do so. There also still is faith in God's ability to change the hearts of men to do what is right and just. After all, all things are possible with God.

"Slavery is theft—theft of a life, theft of work, theft of any property or produce, theft even of the children a slave might have borne."

Kevin Bales

1
America's Modern-Day Slaves

THE 13TH AMENDMENT to the United States Constitution explicitly prohibited slavery in every form. Also, the Civil Right Legislation of 1964 was enacted to end discrimination against Americans based on race, color, religion, sex, or national origin. Yet today, in the 21st century, slavery of another form is as pervasive as that which was in place before passage of the 13th Amendment. You may question such a statement in this enlightened age in which we live, but the truth is that slavery still exists.

Examine the definition of "slavery", and you will see what I mean. "Slavery" is defined as a legal or economic system in which principles of law allow individuals to be classified as property to be owned and shackled in chains and bought by the highest bidder. While enslaved, the owner is entitled to the productivity of the slave's labor without any remuneration. True, the modern-day slave may not be owned by an individual and may not wear shackles around his neck or ankles, but that person nonetheless is still a slave.

How do modern-day slaves look? To the outward eye, they look just like you and me. They represent every ethnic and racial group, but they are disproportionately African American. They rely on government welfare systems and handouts to provide for their basic needs. They are tied to a system that keeps them in poverty and encourages them to beg for the crumbs off of the master's—the government's—table. They are people who merely exist. They are fed and lodged, when such resources are available, by the government or through community-run shelters. Those who have their own housing often live in dwellings that are almost uninhabitable, located in forgotten and blighted neighborhoods. They often represent generations of families who have existed in poverty and who have depended upon the government for financial support. They have surrendered control over their destiny to a system that now controls how much they can eat, where and with whom they can live, and how much income they can earn.

In addition, they struggle within a system that does not offer a clear pathway to self-sufficiency or economic independence. The poorer they are, the more invisible they are to many of us, and the harder their lives and their struggle to subsist. Their dreams and aspirations disappear, and their hopes for a happy life are lost. Not metal, but poverty, has chained them and, just like those who are physically enslaved, they see no way out. The American Dream doesn't exist for them. As a result, some succumb to the use of illicit drugs and alcohol to numb the reality of their existence. Others resort to criminal behavior and either terrorize the neighborhoods from which they come or are in jails and prisons nationwide.

The irony is that America is one the wealthiest nations in the world; yet, far too many of its citizens live in poverty and substandard conditions. America leads the world in just about everything that is good; yet, based on the 2012 Census report, more than 45 million people— or 14.5% of all Americans—live below the poverty level. According to the Organization for Economic Cooperation and Development, the U.S. child poverty rate is the highest in the developed world. America works hard at reducing poverty globally, while hiding its own poverty—seeking to make it invisible to the world. However, for some who live in America, the poor are visible every day. We see them daily struggling to make ends meet—with or without jobs, on the street, in shelters—and grappling with growing mental health conditions and drug abuse issues.

There is nothing good that stems from poverty. It is a curse. I do not believe that God intended for His creation to live in poverty. Poverty is evil; it causes pain, criminal behavior, depression, and oppression. When we look at the Bible, God gives us an answer to poverty. The answer is work; that is, if we are physically and mentally able, we are to work. If we cannot work, then the church is called to take care of the poor through tithes and offerings. Scripture tells us that, if a man does not work, he should not eat and that laziness will lead to a life of poverty (Proverbs 6:10-11). There is no substitute for hard work among the able-bodied but, when people are denied the opportunity to work due to race, gender, or religion, it is against God's will for humanity. The Bible says that it is the thief who comes to steal, kill, and destroy, but Jesus came to give life and life more abundantly (John 10:10). Well, poverty steals, kills, and destroys. It steals dreams and ambitions; it kills self-worth; and it destroys lives.

"The burden of poverty isn't just that you don't always have the things you need, it's the feeling of being em-barrassed every day of your life, and you'd do anything to lift that burden."

Jay-Z

2
Everyday Struggles of Modern-Day Slaves

IN THIS CHAPTER, I want us to take a deeper look at the poor in America and their daily struggles. Note that most of the discussion will deal with poor African Americans and their circumstances, but know that much of this discussion is equally reflective of any racial group whose human rights and spirits are being crushed by poverty.

Before we move into the heart of this discussion, though, let me give you some context for why I am so passionate about the poor and the homeless. About 5 years ago, as a Senior Public Health Advisor for the Federal Government, I was invited to speak at an annual luncheon for the homeless program in Miami, Florida. The president of the organization took me on a tour of the homeless shelter facilities, where hundreds of men, women, and children resided. I was humbled as I talked with people and heard their stories. I was drawn to their eyes and their facial expressions; their eyes were desolate, and their faces were filled with sadness and hopelessness. I thought that, had it not been for the grace of God, I could very well have been one of them. One of the bright moments, however, was my visit to their daycare center. The children appeared untouched by these circumstances; they were full of joy, clean, and a wonder to behold. As I watched, I pondered what would happen to them. Would they too live in poverty and become homeless as their parents? My chest became tight, and I began to tear up. I knew that somehow our government and America's churches were not doing enough to help alleviate this problem. When I left this program to fly home, I knew that my thoughts about the poor and reactions to them would be forever changed.

Years later, I was privileged to visit another program for the homeless in Georgia—a housing village for homeless women and children. This community provided apartments for women and children and also opportunities for employment. It was there that I realized my next life assignment—in some way, I was being called to improve the human condition of women and children affected by poverty.

After my retirement from public service, I stepped out in faith and used my resources and retirement savings to establish a transitional housing program for homeless women and children. It was there that my journey began. I was able to get a glimpse into the struggles of women and children living without the necessities of life—food, shelter, and the opportunity to earn living wages. It was there that I began to understand the challenges of people living in poverty. Often we do not recognize the poor when we see them because they look like you and me. They aren't necessarily the homeless that we see sleeping on the streets or standing on corners, but they still are men, women, and children struggling every day to survive.

Often poverty has a female face. She wakes up wondering if the struggle will ever end, and she tries to figure how to make ends meet. Her thoughts are not on buying a car or a house or on taking a vacation; her thoughts go to whether she will have enough money to feed her children today. Will there be enough to buy Johnny shoes? Will the lights be turned off? Will there be an eviction notice on the door, or her belongings stacked outside, because there wasn't enough to pay the rent? It is a constant juggling act to determine which bills to pay first. For most, the thought of asking for help is humiliating and dehumanizing. Because of that, it is not uncommon for them to go without so their children can have food. They suffer in silence and isolation, putting on a good face and not wanting anyone to know that they, or their children, are hungry. They worry about everyday things that would be quite unsettling for most of us.

Many of these women are the working poor, earning less than the minimum wage. Others are welfare recipients, some who have grown up in the system and who now rely on government assistance either to supplement their incomes or to meet their basic needs, as did generations before.

The challenge is that government assistance may not be sufficient. I remember one woman serving her child cookies for breakfast because her food stamps had run out and that was all she had left. Often the poor, especially women, feel powerless over their circumstances and the future, and they become conditioned to believe that the only way to survive is through dependence on a government check to feed their families. When that happens, government support actually becomes a hindrance to self-sufficiency and economic independence. Instead of providing temporary support as intended, it becomes an albatross, standing in the way of the poor moving from poverty to a living-wage job. It is important to note that the government was never intended to provide the necessities of life.

Please know that I am not against government aid or services to the poor. I recognize that people fall on hard times and need assistance. In those instances, services should be there. The problem occurs in continuing to provide aid for decades and not providing the opportunity for job training or access to living-wage jobs. For many African Americans, this has been the case.

African Americans are disproportionately affected by poverty—more than any racial or ethnic group in America. They represent about 12% of the nation's population but have a poverty rate of 27.4%—the highest among America's racial and ethnic groups. What contributes to such a disproportionate poverty rate?   Two critical contributing factors are incarceration and unemployment. Although African Americans make up roughly 12% of the U.S. population, African-American males represent 35% of prison inmates—that is, African-American males are approximately 770,000 of the 2.2 million male inmates, according to 2014 Bureaus of Justice Statistics data.

There are more than 1.1 million absent fathers and more than 120,000 absent mothers impacting millions of children. One in 9 African-American children has a parent in prison, compared to 1 in 57 white children. As a result, high incarceration among African Americans is one factor leading to single-parent homes. Today, 53% of African-American children have only a mother in the home. Again, although only about 12% of the total U.S. population, African Americans account for 25% of the nation's single-parent homes. This is more than twice the percentage of white single-parent families. Whether caused by incarceration or otherwise, single-parent homes impact the economic status of families, their well-being, and children's financial security.

Further exacerbating the problem of poverty among African Americans is unemployment. In many cases, because African Americans have not been able to overcome discrimination in education and employment, they continue to bear the brunt of institutional and economic slavery. For instance, African-American males over age 20 have the highest unemployment rate of any ethnic or racial group—11% compared to 4.4% for white men. Those seeking to re-enter society after prison often find it even more difficult to find employment because they must couple a criminal record with a lack of employable skills and education. Thus, unemployment is a significant contributing factor to African-American poverty in America.

Clearly not all African-Americans struggle economically. Nor would it be accurate to hold that all whites and all other non-black minorities have it made. There are other frequent faces among the poor and enslaved—Hispanics, youth who have aged out of the foster care system, and young human-trafficking victims, among others. Nonetheless, what appears true from the data is that, as a group, African Americans may not have a fair share of the opportunities necessary for a successful life.

No one, of any race or economic status, wants to be enslaved and at the mercy of others. Unfortunately, many in our nation's poor find themselves in just that condition. They have become slaves of poverty and, unwittingly, the slave master for many is the government.

"We live in the richest country in the world. There's plenty to spare and enough for no man, woman, or child to be in want. And, in addition to this, our country was founded on what should have been a great true principle—the freedom, equality, and rights of each individual. Huh! And what has come of this start? There are corporations worth billions of dollars—and hundreds of thousands of people who don't get to eat."

Carlson McCullers

3

The Federal War on Poverty

IN 1929, THE Great Depression plunged the United States into the worst economic downturn in its history. The nation's money supplies diminished; companies went bankrupt and began to fire their workers in droves. By 1932—one of the bleakest years of the Great Depression—at least one-quarter of the American workforce was unemployed. When President Franklin Roosevelt took office in 1933, he acted swiftly to try and stabilize the economy and provide jobs and relief to those who were suffering. Over the next 8 years, the government instituted a series of projects and programs, known collectively as "the New Deal". These programs aimed to restore some measure of dignity and prosperity to the hardest-hit Americans. More than that, Roosevelt's New Deal permanently changed the Federal Government's relationship to the people of the U.S. When Roosevelt later signed the Social Security Act of 1935 into law, it was intended to be a temporary measure. His feeling was that "the Federal Government must and shall quit this business of relief.... Continued dependence upon relief induces a spiritual and moral disintegration, fundamentally destructive to the national fiber."

In 1964, President Lyndon Johnson signed a bill to eliminate poverty, expand educational opportunities, increase the safety net for the poor and unemployed, and meet the health and financial needs of the elderly. Johnson saw the aim of the bill as not only relieving the symptoms of poverty but as curing it. What became known as "the War on Poverty" had two central objectives. One focus was to provide jobs and training, especially for young people who were growing up in poverty and who lacked economic opportunities to keep them from moving fully into the workforce. A second emphasis was to reverse the cycle of poverty in communities at the local level by beginning a planning and organizing process that would bring resources to the community.

These programs were intended to serve as stepping stones to move the poor forward to lives of economic independence and self-sufficiency, and they did indeed supply resources to many needy Americans. Social Security and food stamps, for instance, helped millions in the early years of those programs. However, the programs proved not to be the cure hoped for. Communities still faced many social problems, and poverty remained one of the primary issues facing many in the nation.

Chief among the anti-poverty programs was welfare. Prior to the 1950s, white women and their children were the primary recipients of welfare. Very few African Americans received welfare benefits. Instead, African Americans were more likely to rely on immediate and extended family members to care for them when they fell on hard times. However, in the 1960s that practice began to change. The country's shift from an agrarian society to one based on manufacturing forever changed the skills needed to secure stable employment, leaving many African Americans behind. Those who were skilled often were barred from unions and coveted factory work. Others, though highly capable laborers, often were unable to transfer their skills to white collar clerical and service-oriented jobs. The situation was widespread and impacted generations and communities. Hence, the safety net, historically found through family assistance, disappeared for many African Americans and drove them to seek help from the government.

Unfortunately, the public assistance system, which was ostensibly in place to help families, did just the opposite in reality. Under the system, unemployed husbands and significant others were not allowed to stay with their families; in fact, welfare workers, like myself, were told to deny benefits to a family if there was evidence of a man in the house. In other words, in order to be eligible for welfare, a woman had to deny that her husband or her children's father was in the home. This practice of intact family denial was a significant factor in the breakdown of the African-American family. The result was that, all too often, African-American men found themselves not only without the work opportunities and financial resources to take care of their families themselves, but their limited financial situation forced a critical choice—openly participate in the life of the family and risk its loss of benefits or either stay away or hide in order to keep the family on government assistance and afloat.

Welfare policies did not just discourage marriage and the formation of stable families; they also negatively affected the development of a healthy work ethic. As Heritage Foundation scholar Michael Franc noted in 2012:

> "[T]he necessity of phasing out [welfare] benefits, as incomes rise, brings a serious moral hazard. In many cases, economists have calculated [that] welfare recipients who enter the work force or receive pay raises lose a dollar or more of benefits for each additional dollar they earn. The system makes fools of those who work hard."

In testimony on Capitol Hill, Rep. Geoff Davis (R-Kentucky) concurred. He noted that, although federal welfare programs "are designed to alleviate poverty while promoting work," collectively they have "an unintended side effect of discouraging harder work and higher earnings. The more benefits the government provides, the stronger the disincentive to work." Most people on welfare work; however, the jobs they hold pay less than living wages. It isn't the unemployed that strain the welfare system, as you would think; it is the working poor, according to researchers from the University of California, Berkley. Their studies show that the majority of households receiving government assistance are headed by a working adult.

So what is the government to do to change this trajectory for the poor? The answers may be these: creating living-wage jobs and then providing job training so individuals are equipped with the necessary skills to fill them; funding affordable day care, child development centers, afterschool activities, and after-hours or night care programs to relieve the financial burden and concerns related to safe, quality child care for working families; increasing the number of affordable houses; and actively seeking out private-sector partnerships to offset government costs to fund and operate such programs.

"The greatest obstacle to the welfare state is not greed but private charity that makes the welfare state irrelevant; the greatest obstacle to re-education of children in the name of the collective is allegiance to a higher power. More than that, the greatest obstacle to the state as god is an actual God above the state."

Ben Shapiro

4

The Church's Call to Care for the Poor

THE CHURCH HAS always had a mandate from God to care for the poor. The individual is also mandated by Scripture to work if able. The Bible charges the individual who has the ability to work to do so (1 Thessalonians 4:11; 2 Thessalonians 3:10). Nowhere in Scripture will you find God instructing the government to care or provide for the poor. When people are unable to provide for themselves, it is the church's responsibility to step in. The Message Bible describes the church's responsibility this way:

> "This is how we've come to understand and experience love: Christ sacrificed His life for us. This is why we ought to live sacrificially for our fellow believers, and not just be out for ourselves. If we see some brother or sister in need and have means to do something about it but turn a cold shoulder and do nothing, what happens to God's love? It disappears. And you made it disappear." (1 John 3:16-17)."

Throughout Scripture, we find God addressing the church's responsibility about caring for the poor. According to pastor and author Rick

Warren, there are 2,000 Bible verses that deal with the issue of the poor. In fact, the term "poor" appears more than 300 times in the King James translation.

We repeatedly see God's care and concern for the poor and struggling. We see this focus in both the Old and New Testaments. Here are a few examples from the New International Version:

- "Do not deprive the foreigner or the fatherless of justice, or take the cloak of a widow as a pledge." (Deuteronomy 24:17)
- "Speak up for those who cannot speak for themselves, for the rights of all who are destitute. Speak up and judge fairly; defend the rights of the poor and needy." (Proverbs 31:8-9)
- "I rescued the poor who cried out for help, and the fatherless who had none to assist them." (Job 29:12)
- "If anyone has material possessions and sees a brother or sister in need but has no pity on them, how can the love of God be in that person?" (1 John 3:17)
- "Suppose a brother or sister is without clothes and daily food. If one of you says to them, 'Go in peace; keep warm and well fed,' but does nothing about their physical needs, what good is it?" (James 2:15-16)
- "Jesus answered, 'If you want to be perfect, go, sell your possessions and give to the poor, and you will have treasure in heaven. Then come, follow me.'" (Matthew 19:21)
- "The Spirit of the Lord is on me because He has anointed me to proclaim good news to the poor. He has sent me to proclaim freedom for the prisoners and recovery of sight for the blind, to set the oppressed free." (Luke 4:18)
- "But when you give a banquet, invite the poor, the crippled, the lame, the blind, and you will be blessed. Although they cannot repay you, you will be repaid at the resurrection of the righteous." (Luke 14:13)

Churches and faith-based organizations in America have played a critical role in responding to the needs of the poor. The early church established most of the social services programs and educational institutions that functioned throughout our history. The church was very generous in sharing what it had with the poor, usually poor believers. However, that helping role diminished dramatically with the expansion of government programs, beginning with the New Deal of the 1930s. As the government's role increased with regard to providing for the poor and the unemployed, the church's charitable activities and giving decreased. Yet, in recent years, starting with the passage of what's known as the "Charitable Choice" legislation of the 1990s, faith-based organizations have been called on to increase their efforts to assist the poor by partnering with the government to provide social services to the addicted, homeless, prisoners, elderly, and at-risk children. The government has supported these efforts through grants, contracts, and technical assistance to support faith-based groups to improve their service delivery systems, strengthen program capacity, and encourage positive outcomes.

During my last 11 years of public service for the government as a Federal Liaison for Faith-Based Issues, I had the opportunity to work with faith-based organizations and faith leaders across the country to help them stabilize their service offerings and expand their ability to assist the poor and disadvantaged. To be honest, there were some leaders who seemed more interested in securing grant money to fund charitable initiatives so that they did not have to use the church's financial resources from the tithes and offerings of their congregants. I think those leaders missed the mark biblically. Regardless of government financial support to fund services for the poor, the Church of Jesus Christ has a mandate from God to provide for the poor—widows, strangers, and the fatherless (Deuteronomy 14:28-29).

The truth is that most of the revenue that churches receive does not serve the needs of the poor. U.S. congregations in 2014 devoted less than 10% of their annual revenue for poverty-related services and supports, as reported by the National Center for Charitable Statistics. According to that body, religious organizations received about $114.68 billion in revenue in 2014. Of that amount, most was spent on salaries, mortgages for buildings, and other material supplements to the ministry. Less than 5% of the national church revenue amount was allocated to benevolence activities. While it's disheartening that churches overall are giving very little to the cause of the poor, there are churches of various denominations and faith-based organizations that are answering the call of Christ concerning the poor and doing great work.

As the church, we have been called to minister and provide for the least of these. Certainly, we are called to preach the good news to the poor, but our charge doesn't stop there. We also have a fiduciary responsibility, as Christ's ambassadors, to be the hands and feet of Jesus in meeting the needs of children; those in prison; and those needing food, clothing, and shelter. We are to demonstrate the heart and love of God to a fallen world. Jesus was very clear with His disciples on this point.

> "For I was hungry and you gave me something to eat, I was thirsty and you gave me something to drink, I was a stranger and you invited me in, I needed clothes and you clothed me, I was sick and you looked after me, I was in prison and you came to visit me. Then the righteous will answer Him, 'Lord when did we see you hungry and feed you, or thirsty and give you something to drink? When did we see you a stranger and invite you in, or needing clothes and clothe you? When did we see you sick or when in prison go visit you?' The King will reply, 'Truly I tell you, whatever you did for one of the least of these brothers and sisters of mine, you did for me.'" (Matthew 25:35-40, NIV)

Today, as never before, it is time for the church to step up and become a defense, a beacon of hope, and a refuge, especially for the poor and those who have lost their way. And, for no group is that more needed than for children. There are countless children waiting for the church. These are the children who are living in impoverished circumstances—children living in America's shelters, children whose parents are unable to meet their daily needs or to do so consistently, children who have been forced to grow up before their time. These are children who live in a home with drug-addicted parents or parents with mental health conditions. These are children who are without parents or who have been removed from their homes for their wellbeing and now are in the nation's foster care system. These are the fatherless and motherless that God has called us to care for.

As the church, are we willing to care for them as God commands? There are ways in which the church can play a critical role in changing the trajectory of these children's lives, such as by becoming adoptive parents, foster parents, or spiritual parental surrogates. The church can rescue them from the hand of the enemy, give them hope, provide for their needs as appropriate, and show them a better way of life. Jesus' concern for children should be ours as well. The Bible tells us that "Jesus said, 'Let the children come to Me, and do not hinder them, for the kingdom of Heaven belongs to such as these'" (Matthew 19:14, NIV). How will the children come to Jesus if the church does not offer them the door to God's kingdom?

Being the church is more than providing spiritual activities for the congregation or different kinds of church services and programs. This is not to say that such programming is not important or that it is not good work for Christ's church. But, we have a higher calling—a calling to proclaim the gospel of freedom to the world by demonstrating the love of Christ to the poor, by caring for them, by making disciples, and by teaching them the value of hard work and dependence on

God—the One who is the true provider of all of their needs. We have been assigned to win the hearts of the poor, to assist them with the discovery and fulfillment of their purpose, to help them regain their human dignity, to teach them the ways of God, to empower them to be self-sufficient, and to prepare them to be hard workers. It is our responsibility to care as Jesus cared. The church has been called to be the protector and defender of the poor. In the Book of Isaiah, we are instructed:

> "If you spend yourselves in behalf of the hungry and satisfy the needs of the oppressed, your light will rise in the darkness, and your night will become like the noonday. The Lord will guide you always; He will satisfy your needs in a sun-scorched land and will strengthen your frame. You will be like a well-watered garden; like a spring whose waters never fail." (Isaiah 58:10-11 NIV)

The Message Bible translation records the same passage this way:

> "If you are generous with the hungry and start giving your-selves to the down-and out, [y]our lives will begin to glow in the darkness, your shadowed lives will be bathed in sunlight. I will always show you where to go. I'll give you a full life in the emptiest of places—firm muscles, strong bones. You'll be like a well-watered garden, a gurgling spring that never runs dry."

God's desire is to end suffering and injustice. He demonstrated this by freeing the oppressed Israelites from Egyptian bondage (Exodus 3:7-8). He is concerned when people are enslaved or oppressed. He is the liberator of the oppressed and the poor. Through the prophet Amos, God condemned the oppression of the poor by the wealthy in the northern kingdom of Israel (Amos 4:1); while Isaiah denounced the maltreatment of the poor in the southern kingdom of Judah

(Isaiah 10:1-3). The prophet Micah condemned those in Judah who "covet fields and seize them; and houses, and take them. They defraud a man of his home, a fellowman of his inheritance" (Micah 2:2). A century later Jeremiah denounced the rich who exploited the poor (Jeremiah 5:26-29).

Jesus' mission was to set the oppressed free and restore the sight of the blind. His heart leaned towards the poor—healing the sick and feeding the hungry (Luke 4:18-19). As Jesus did so should we, as His church. We must feed the hungry, clothe the naked, visit the prisoner, and provide shelter for the homeless.

This is our call, Church. Will you answer it?

"Across our country, social enterprise partnerships between the public and private sectors are providing millions of Americans—young and old—a second chance."

George R. Brown

5

The Role of Private Sector
Partnerships in Alleviating Poverty

THE ANSWER TO breaking the chains that bind people to poverty and economic slavery has always been found in education and job creation. It is a major path out of poverty. In the years after the emancipation of U.S. slaves, black and white teachers from the North and South, missionary organizations, churches, and schools worked tirelessly to give former slaves the opportunity to learn. And, the newly freed took advantage of the opportunity to become literate. Grandparents and their grandchildren sat together in classrooms seeking to obtain the tools of freedom. After learning to read, African Americans during this period were able to vote, actively participate in the political process, acquire the land of former owners, seek their own employment, and use public accommodations. This is why, even today, education and employment are viewed as the tools to freedom—freedom that allows every man and woman to become educated and to secure employment that will lead to self-sufficiency.

It is true that people, who are without education and who are unskilled, are less likely to become gainfully employed because they lack the education and skills to fill available jobs. Therefore, the lack of education impairs a person's earning power. For example, the average African American with some form of higher education will earn at least $9,142 more in annual income than a high-school drop-out. Not only are incomes increased when people are educated, they also become empowered. No matter what our responses are regarding America's poverty, it boils down to education and creating jobs so people can work. This is why, today, education and job creation is at the center of all discussions about alleviating poverty in the United States and globally. Poor people do want to work, regardless of what we think. They want to have the financial means to take care of themselves and their families. Some may appear intellectually limited, but there are still jobs available that they can be trained to do to earn a living wage.

Look at the post-slavery period. It was the will of the people, working together, and education that brought about true freedom for the former slaves. One African proverb says that "[i]t takes a village to raise a child," and this is true. It also takes a village to eradicate poverty and to build healthy and economically sound communities.

The private sector—corporations, foundations, and businesses—can play a significant role in achieving the end to poverty by working with the government and communities at the local level. These partners are valuable resources and have the capacity to aid community development, enhance human and public services, revitalize and rebuild communities, and improve the lives of people residing in them. They have a social responsibility to the community that goes beyond providing goods and services.

The private sector is in a unique position to contribute to the economy of the community. It can create jobs, offer training opportunities, and employ community members to meet workforce demands. Businesses become intricately tied to both the community and government and are able to work together with them to solve the complex issues that communities face. This is a mutually beneficial partnership that not only provides a structure for sharing information, enhancing technical resources, and strengthening relationships, but it also serves as a vehicle from which substantial amounts of money can be delivered to support community initiatives, such as job creation and training, minority small-business support, affordable housing, child care, and the like.

Partnerships of this kind also can help develop and finance apprenticeships, job-skill training, and job-matching programs. Such partnerships have the ability to stimulate economic growth, create jobs, build infrastructure, and strengthen the economic base for public expenditures as well as increase earning capacity and lift individuals out of poverty.

"A host of positive psychological changes inevitably will result from widespread economic security. The dignity of the individual will flourish when the decisions concerning his life are in his own hands, when he has the assurance that his income is stable and certain, and when he knows that he has the means to seek improvement."

Martin Luther King, Jr.

6

Individual and Family Responsibility

THUS FAR, WE have focused on the responsibility of the government, the church, and the private sector to the poor and on how those institutions may, or may not, contribute to alleviating poverty among people in America's neighborhoods and communities. In these sections, though, there has been limited discussion about the role that individuals and family can play in alleviating poverty.

Personal Responsibility
I believe it is the desire of every person to be able to take care of self and family. People want a living-wage job to support their families. However, because of economic inequities, lack of appropriate job skills, and sometimes racism, many are denied the opportunity to work. For some, this disconnect between desire and reality stems from an inability to secure living-wage jobs. I agree with Melissa Boteach, the Director of the Poverty and Prosperity Program at the Center for American Progress: "The best ticket out of poverty is a good job. For working age adults, people have a responsibility to look for work and support themselves. In turn, we have a responsibility to make sure there are opportunities to do that and that we're removing barriers to work."

We talked a bit about God's call for the church to care for those who cannot care for themselves. It is important to note that the Bible does not, and neither should we, overlook an individual's responsibility for his or her own life. The Bible teaches that each of us is to function responsibly—we are to engage in work activities (Genesis 2:15; 1 Thessalonians 4:11), use our resources wisely (Proverbs 10:5), and be diligent (Proverbs 10:4, 12:24, and 22:29). This may mean studying while others are having fun. It may mean taking advantage of remedial education and job-training programs to improve readiness for work. It may mean accepting less-than-glamorous jobs in order to gain experience, build a work history, and earn an honest income. It may mean delaying pregnancy until able to provide the basic necessities for a family.

Although the circumstances may differ, being responsible for one's own care is the first step. We are to do our best to care for ourselves so that we don't have to look to others to take care of us. When individuals are willing to take personal responsibility and work hard, they should be given the necessary support and training, and natural partnership should occur between them and government, church, and community.

Personal responsibility and self-determination, coupled with education and training, are the quickest ways to break the cycle of poverty. God expects us to work. In Genesis 2:15 it says, "[t]he Lord God took the man and put him in the Garden of Eden to work it and keep it." Ephesians 4:28 (MSG) says this: "Did you use to make ends meet by stealing? Well, no more! Get an honest job so that you can help others who can't work". Further, Proverbs 12:11 (TLB) states that "[h]ard work means prosperity; only a fool idles away his time".

Family Responsibility
The second aspect of personal responsibility is seeking to attend to the needs of one's own family. Scripture says that "[i]f anyone does not provide for his own, and especially for those of his household, he has denied the faith and is worse than an unbeliever" (1 Timothy 5:8,

NKJV). While everyone in a person's immediate family is covered by this verse, it is especially important for each of us to ensure that children—perhaps the most vulnerable family members—are cared for.

Every child should be safe and secure; every child should have food, clothing, shelter, education, and love to grow and develop. Research shows that children raised in stable, secure families have a better chance to flourish. The expectation is that the child's parents or guardians have the necessary resources to achieve this. You see, providing for children isn't initially a government responsibility; it is first an individual one.

Children learn at home how to live and take care of themselves. It is the family that has the primary responsibility to provide the material and emotional support to each child in its care. Also, it is the family that is to make decisions regarding quality education for the child so that he can learn, develop, and obtain the skills and knowledge to survive in the world. A child's well-being and success in life are tied to the care that is given by his parents and/or extended family.

Studies have shown that children who grow up in two-parent homes generally fare better in terms of high-school completion, college attendance, and the ability to secure good paying jobs than their counterparts from one-parent homes. In contrast, single-mother households experience special difficulty in ensuring that their children's basic needs are met, and this is the group most likely to depend upon government programs for help. By definition, single-mother households do not have a spouse or significant other to provide financial or emotional support and, as noted previously, the system discourages efforts to develop or reestablish two-adult families, by denying or decreasing welfare benefits or housing subsidies when a man is in the home, even if the family continues to struggle economically. With 35% of African-American men incarcerated and 49% unemployed, it is not surprising that African Americans account for the largest number of single-mother households in the U.S. and have the highest rate of single-mother households receiving some type of public aid. These factors alone explain why 46% of African-American families live in poverty.

The term "family" does not apply only to the members of one's own household, however. The extended family can, and should, play a critical role in assisting those who are unable to care for themselves fully. Serving as a resource, especially for the family's children, extended family members can offer support in ways that parents may not.

For instance, it is important for families to lend a hand to provide some level of care for the children of parents affected by drug addiction, mental health disorders, or incarceration. Unfortunately, too often, these children are abandoned and placed into the foster care system. While Scripture commands the church to help the orphans and the fatherless, it is first the family's responsibility to care for these children whenever possible. However, assuming or sharing care is quite challenging for some families because they too have limited finances and other resources.

I remember, though, when I was a young girl, our home was always open to helping extended family—actual relatives and friends—get back on their feet during hard times, often until they were gainfully employed. Our home was a place of refuge for many. It was there that I learned about God, the wonderful plans that He has for us, and how He wants us to share His love with others. In my home I first learned that it is difficult for children to thrive without the input and influence of family—the people who are supposed to instill faith, hope, and encouragement so that children can both dream and succeed.

According to the Brookings Institute, if America truly believes that children of all races need stable and secure homes with two loving and nurturing parents, then fathers need to be taken seriously. When fathers are employed, and when they are living in or connected to the home, they are able to contribute financially and otherwise to the whole family's wellbeing.

Improving family life in America means that men and women should be able to secure living-wage jobs, receive a good education, and have the opportunity to participate in job training and skill-development programs that prepare them for the demands of the current workforce. There is an unmistakable relationship between family, employment, education, and poverty. If we are to break the intergenerational cycle of poverty, then men and women—fathers and mothers—must have the opportunity to work and earn a reasonable living so that they can become the primary family income source and will be in a position to offer the other aspects of care needed to nurture the family.

I believe that individuals and families can lift themselves out of poverty by working hard at what already has been placed in their hands, as did my parents and generations before, even if sometimes with help. Extended families and a person's network may contribute also by supplying or supplementing financial, food, childcare, or other resources to help that family get on its feet.

There are many among us who need our help and support. Many are trying to assume personal responsibility and find a way out of poverty, but the pathway is littered with roadblocks. Everyone should have the chance to realize the American Dream, and there is a part for each of us to play in helping them to do so.

"I know that government doesn't have all the solutions and that real solutions do not come from the top down. Instead, the ways to end poverty come from all of us. We are part of the solution."

Kathleen Blanco

7

The Last Word and Moving Forward

SO WHAT CAN we do to reduce poverty in our neighborhoods and communities? The answer to this question lands in the laps of the individual, the family, the government, the community, and the church. There is a need for a collaborative effort among all of these groups. It is not trite; it really does take a village, working together, to nurture future generations and save them from poverty.

Although President Lyndon Johnson declared an end to the war on poverty over 50 years ago, today we still are wrestling mightily with poverty and its impact on families and neighborhoods in America. We have more families on the welfare rolls than at any time in history, and this rise is likely to continue unless we take strategic steps to eradicate poverty for the good in our country. We have the financial resources, ingenuity, and manpower to achieve this, but we must also have the will.

Additionally, as we engage in a dialogue around problem solving and as we seek to develop effective strategies, it is essential to have those most intimately affected—the poor—at the table. We cannot continue to make policy and program decisions for people without their voice. Those, who have never experienced poverty or received government welfare benefits, should not assume that they have all of the answers. To encourage understanding, and also to empower people, they should have the opportunity to tell their own stories, provide feedback about the system, and contribute to the discussion about what is needed to move a person from poverty to self-sufficiency and economic independence.

While writing this book, I've read a great deal of literature about how to resolve our country's poverty issues. Opinions vary. There are calls for women not to have children before they marry; beliefs that anyone who is poor should be able to secure full-time employment; recommendations that government expect welfare recipients to make reasonable efforts to comply with program requirements, rewarding those who do and punishing those who don't; and suggestions that the whole matter would be resolved if the poor were to get a good education.

Honestly, I think that much of the analysis is a bit shortsighted, especially for African-American families. There is a range of complex factors that contribute to the situation. For instance, getting a good education in many inner-city neighborhoods is nearly impossible because of the poor performance of schools there. Poverty in these neighborhoods is impacted by the frequent failure of women to marry before childbirth and also by the significant number of men who are unemployed or incarcerated. Marrying someone who is unemployed and incarcerated does not lift a family from poverty; this occurs only when a woman marries a man who earns a living wage. And, the ability to earn a living wage is directly tied to education—one's ability to acquire the knowledge and job skills that the labor market demands.

In 1931, writer James Truslow Adams coined the term "the American Dream". His vision of the desire held by people throughout our country is as true today as it was decades ago. Americans still dream of a land in which life should be better, richer, and fuller for everyone. It still should be a land of opportunity for each person, according to his or her ability or achievement. That dream really is the dream of all Americans, irrespective of their race, social class, or home state.

If we choose to ignore the plight of the poor, America itself will be as responsible for the lost sense of security and purpose—for the destroyed self-esteem, self-worth, human dignity, and hope for the future—as are the people who fail to exercise personal responsibility. If America's actions, or its inaction, perpetuate a life of unending poverty for poor children, there will be no pathway for them to become self-sufficient and take charge of their futures.

Not all who are poor are lazy and unproductive. Many sincerely want a better future for themselves and their children. America has the opportunity to become an effective resource for the poor by putting into place policies and programs that will end the cycle, help lift people out of the chokehold of poverty, and offer opportunity to empower the least of these to become viable contributors and productive citizens.

The question is, "How?" How do we address the problem of poverty in America? Let me repeat that it takes the concerted effort of the government, church, community, family, and individual. Nothing short of us all working together will bring about the type of change needed.

From my perspective, let me offer some specific recommendations for each of these essential participants in the important work of eradicating poverty in our country.

What can government and the private sector do?

- Work towards ensuring that there are ample jobs for people at all skill levels.
- Implement urban renewal and revitalization programs for poor neighborhoods to make them attractive to developers and investors in order to create opportunities for employment and for affordable, quality housing in such neighborhoods.
- Promote quality public education from kindergarten to high school to prepare students for community and four-year colleges as well as for trade and apprenticeship programs to bolster education in all areas of the country.
- Commit appropriate resources so that current and future workers receive job training and retraining that will equip them with the knowledge and skills necessary for the constantly evolving job market.
- Finance community learning centers in poor neighborhoods to promote job training and apprenticeship programming to increase employment opportunities.
- Commit to public-private partnerships to finance community initiatives, create jobs, and offer on-the-job training opportunities.
- Encourage entrepreneurship.
- Work towards developing, implementing, and enforcing policies that combat racial discrimination in employment and in housing.

What can the church do?

As followers of Jesus, if we are to live out our biblical mandate, we are compelled to address the issue of poverty. The church is called to be Christ's ambassadors—His hands—showing His heart to those He has called "the least of these". The Church of Jesus Christ is rich in resources—time, energy, finances, knowledge, skills, and of course, the gospel. Here are some of the ways the church may participate in eradicating poverty in America.

- Recognize that discipleship is one of the most important tools available to address poverty.
- Help people believe in themselves and discover their vision and passions.
- Provide outreach to the poor and homeless; treat those in need with respect and dignity.
- Become a community network center to help people identify available community resources.
- Roll up your sleeves, get dirty, and follow God's command to feed, clothe, and shelter the poor. This means helping the poor until they get on their feet and being a support spiritually and emotionally as they work their way out of poverty.
- Solicit and train volunteers to be mentors, tutors, and parental surrogates for poor children.
- Encourage foster and adoptive parenting among members of the church.
- Dedicate 10% of annual church revenue to services for the poor, or collect a tithe or special offering every 3 years to fund services for the poor.
- Encourage congregants to designate on their tithe and offering envelopes their intention to allocate a specific percentage of the enclosed amount to the poor.
- Use appropriate church space as night shelters for the homeless.
- Establish quality daycare and child-development centers and/ or after-school programs for youth.
- Utilize the church's family-life or community center fully for those in need, as a health center, a satellite social-service location, or a job- or workforce-development site. Grant assistance is available for some of these activities.

- Offer onsite General Education Development (GED) programs.
- Host community college courses or identify speakers from among the members of the congregation to lead classes of interest.
- Implement mentoring programs for children, youth, and/or parents.
- Connect with area shelters to identify children and families at risk and with whom your congregation can develop relationships.
- Offer drug-prevention and spiritual-development activities.
- Identify and join local partnerships of churches and community groups serving the poor and/or youth.
- Purchase and rehabilitate abandoned city properties, converting them into apartments and houses for the poor.
- Establish a volunteer work program, giving the poor the opportunity to earn job experience.
- Become the voice for the poor by serving on advisory boards, workgroups, and committees.
- Help the government to develop and implement policies to improve the lives of the poor.
- Help meet the physical needs of the poor, but do not forget to teach them personal responsibility and ways to become financially independent.

What can individuals and families do?

Families are the primary sources for changing the trajectory of children's lives and impacting future generations. What a family does will ultimately have far-reaching effects on their children's development and on whether or not they will live in poverty. The individual is the starting point in turning his or her situation around. In doing this, the individual must be willing to take personal responsibility for his or her own future, and for the future his children, and to make appropriate life choices.

An individual might start off by asking the following questions: Are we old enough to take on parental responsibility? Are we emotionally mature enough to take care of a child? Do we have the financial resources to bring a child into the world? Can we provide the care and safety a child deserves? If I end up being a single parent, am I in a position to raise a child alone? Do we have a solid support system in place for us, as parents, and for our child?

The following are things that you can do.

- Grow your faith in God and His ability to guide your life and take care of you.
- Stay in school, go back to school, or secure your GED certificate if you have been out of school for a time, so that you have the basic knowledge and skills needed for the workforce.
- Seek out free trade schools that offer certifications in heating and air conditioning, plumbing, and similar highly skilled job areas.
- Enroll in higher education at a college, university, or community college in a course of study that will lead to a degree or certificate.
- Seek out job opportunities each week. Have resumes ready to distribute.
- Model good behavior and a good work ethic for your child.
- Inspire your child's educational pursuits by completing high school, acquiring a GED, or attending college or a certification program yourself.
- Take an interest in your child's schoolwork. Know what he or she is learning.
- Ensure that your child is doing homework. Help as you are able, and seek out free or low-cost tutoring, when needed, so that your child can excel in his or her studies.

- Become active in your child's school by attending parent-teacher conferences, participating in the PTA, volunteering, or otherwise communicating with teachers. You can be the voice for your child and the advocate for his or her quality education.
- Enroll your child in community-sponsored mentoring and enrichment programs that will encourage leadership and character development.
- Take your child to church and/or to faith-based programs to aid in his or her spiritual development.
- Discover social outlets and recreational activities after school or during the summer months. Your child may qualify for free summer camps or enrichment programs. Also, there are many free and low-cost cultural events, museums, parks, and other activities in most areas of the country that you can attend together.
- Invest time with your child. Daily activities, like eating together around the dinner table, reading before bed, or having a movie night, can make a significant difference for your home. These are opportunities to talk together about values, character, purpose, and other daily life matters.

Conclusion

The last words for this chapter are simple. Poverty is not complicated. In this country, there is a need for human kindness. We need a collective recognition that the Founding Fathers really did have it right—all men are created equal and should have access to life, liberty, and the pursuit of happiness. The American Dream should be for all Americans.

Helping others reach the American Dream begins with us. It starts with an adjustment of our hearts and a commitment to become a society that has real concern for the welfare of the poor. Only then can we ensure that our government treats everyone as equals and gives everyone access to the opportunities this country has to offer. The truth, however, is that the government is a reflection of the people it represents. If it is dysfunctional, it is because the people it serves also are dysfunctional in many ways. We are dysfunctional because we may acknowledge the poor among us, but we do very little ourselves, and do not hold responsible those who represent us, to remove the barriers that cause or sustain poverty and dependency.

The heart change regarding poverty also must stir within the church. Why? Because many churches have abdicated their calling from God regarding the poor—a calling spelled out clearly in both Old and New Testaments. Although I reference the Bible, not only Christians are implicated; we, and other faith groups that adhere to similar spiritual teachings, cannot continue to be indifferent to God's commands. There is clear instruction to care for the poor; it is right, and it pleases God.

The family and the individual are not excused from responsibility in changing the trajectory of poverty in America either. Families, and each individual in them, can begin by making wise choices about when they are emotionally and financially ready to provide and care for a child and can postpone becoming parents until they are prepared. People must recognize the importance of education, job training, and hard work in the process of moving out of poverty. Families must understand just how critical children's early years are to their future and invest in helping them to develop their minds and characters during those years. Families must return to the practice of providing support, as they are able, to members of their immediate and extended families during times of need. And, families must recognize that, more than anything else, their faith is the cornerstone of living the American Dream and reaching their God-given destiny.

We must remember what our Founding Fathers stated in the Declaration of Independence. All men are created equal and have a right to pursue happiness and wellbeing. While these statements are true, they are not living truths for many, especially for the poor and disenfranchised who are denied the pursuit of happiness and wellbeing because of their station in life and often their race.

But we, the people—the government, the church, the community, the family, and the individual—working together, can break the chains of poverty that enslave far too many Americans. Each is accountable for doing its part to eradicate poverty. This must be a joint effort with shared responsibility. Only when we each step forward can we turn the corner on poverty in American communities and end America's modern-day slavery. For, we are a nation that God has blessed with resources. We are a nation in which dreams can become a reality, where men and women can embrace a life free of poverty, and where children can grow up knowing that they can be anything that they desire regardless of their race, skin color, or economic status. President Barack Obama captured these thoughts well:

> "We, the People, recognize that we have responsibilities as well as rights; that our destinies are bound together; that a freedom which only asks what's in it for me, a freedom without a commitment to others, a freedom without love or charity or duty or patriotism, is unworthy of our founding ideals, and those who died in their defense."

We are a nation standing tall—one that is a shining light to the world. President Ronald Regan explained in his farewell address to the nation:

"I've spoken of the Shining City all my political life... In my mind it was a tall proud city built on rocks stronger than the oceans, windswept, God-blessed, and teeming with people of all kinds living in peace and harmony; a city with free ports that hummed with commerce and creativity. And if there had to be walls, the walls had doors and doors were open to anyone with the will and heart to get here. That's how I saw it and see it still."

We have a responsibility, as "we the people", to work together to ensure that everyone shares in the American Dream. Everyone deserves the right to succeed; to earn a living wage; and to pursue a life of safety, financial security, and wellbeing.

I close with the words of President Bill Clinton:

"We'll think of the faith of our parents that was instilled in us here in America, the idea that if you work and play by the rules, you'll be rewarded with a good life for yourself and a better chance for your children. Filled with that faith, generations of Americans have worked long hours on their jobs and passed along powerful dreams to their sons and daughters. Many of us can remember our own parents working long hours on their jobs and then coming home and helping us with homework. The American dream has always been a better life for people who are willing to work."

The New American Slave – Not Me!

Who do you say I am?
Where do you say I come from?
Am I not made of the same blood that you are?
Do I not have a mouth to speak?
Do I not have two legs and feet?
Two arms and two hands?
I'm human.
I'm alive.
I'm not invisible.
My skin color may be black, yellow, or white,
Because of this, should I be denied my inalienable rights?
A right to happiness, well-being, and a good life?
I have been made equal by God and in His image, can't you see?
I may not have money, but I have strong hands, and a good mind,
I have the ability to work hard if given the chance,
But, yet today, this life escapes me.
Because I have no income, poverty surrounds me.
I am chained, constrained, and a system controls my life.
I'm like an animal begging for bread;
It's hard for me to see a better life ahead.
No job in site, no strength to fight,

I am the poor,
Dependent on a system to make sure my children are fed.
Who am I?
Do I deserve to live this type of life?
They call me the Modern-Day American Slave.
Someone else controls my life;
I've been denied my human and equal rights.
Not long, I say…. Not long, I say.
For, better times are coming,
For, I am taking personal responsibility,
Preparing myself,
To be all that God has designed me to be.
Don't need a helping hand but a job opportunity,
To work with my hands, to earn a living wage, to take care of my family.
I know that, with my faith in God and Him on my side, Justice will arise.
I will not be denied.
A better life is ahead for me.
A good life calls me.
I will not be denied the opportunity to pursue happiness, well-being, and a good life.
No longer a slave but walking tall,
I'm being loosed from the chains of poverty.
No more an American Slave, but a person of dignity,
With resolve, to live the American Dream, and achieve my God-given destiny.

Poem written by Jocelyn Whitfield

About the Author

Over the last 30 years, Jocelyn Whitfield has worked nationally building the capacities of community and faith-based organizations to serve the poor, needy, and those affected by addictions and mental health conditions. She has been up close and personal in communities, hearing the problems associated with poverty from people in need of social services and their providers. As a result, she has become an advocate for the poor and homeless.

Also, Jocelyn has spent the last 25 years of her life serving in ministries throughout Maryland and continues her ministry to women today. She is an author, a convener of conferences, speaker, and Bible teacher.

Currently, she is the CEO of the Center for Creative Life and Learning, Inc., a 501(c)3 nonprofit organization supporting homeless women and children.

You may contact Jocelyn at jocelyn7266@gmail.com.

Sources, References, and Scriptures

Chapter1: America's Modern-Day Slaves

1. Dan Werner, Fighting Modern Day Slavery, SPLC Poverty Law Center, January 30, 2011
2. CNN, Freedom Project – Ending Modern Day Slavery, March 4, 2011
3. Graziella Bertocchi, Arcangelo Dimici, The Historical Roots of Inequality, November 2010
4. Bureau of Justice Statistics, 2014
5. 2014 Census, Census.gov
6. Feeding America, African American Poverty and Hunger, Fact Sheet, 2016
7. Washington Post News, Black Poverty Differs from White Poverty Among Racial and Ethnic Groups, April 12, 2015
8. Luke 12:33

Chapter 2: Everyday Struggles of Modern-Day Slaves

1. Cincinnati Enquirer, Everyday Struggles of Children Born in Poverty, August 12, 2016
2. Conceiving Children in Poverty Can Be Controlled, August 23, 2016

3. Cincinnati Enquirer, Handouts Are Not Helping Reduce Poverty, August 11, 2016

4. Jeff Madrick, Handouts Are Often Better than a Hand Up, New York Times, April 17, 2016

5. Ben Jarvin, 20 Things the Poor Really Do Every Day that the Rich Never Have to Do, December 5, 2013

6. R. Rector, Heritage Foundation, Understanding Poverty in America, January 8, 2004

7. Genesis 1:1-2, Genesis 2:15

8. 2 Thessalonians 3:10, 1 Thessalonians 4:11

Chapter 3: The Federal War on Poverty

1. New Deal – Facts & Summary,1932

2. Economic Opportunity Act of 1964, Wikipedia

3. Safety Net, NBC News/Wall Street Journal – Nationwide Poll: Income Gap, May 4, 2015

4. Schaefer, Urban Institute, Reshaping the American Workforce in a Changing Economy, 2008

5. Robert Lerman, Center for American Progress, Training American's Workforce and Apprenticeship as Collaborative Routes to Rewarding Careers, December 9, 2009

6. Ben Olinsky and Sarah Ayers, Training for Success: A Policy for Apprenticeships, November 2013.

7. Carolyn J. Hendrich and John Karl Scholz, Making the Work-Based Safety Net Work Better: Forward-Looking Policies to Help Low-Income Families, 2011

8. A. Sherman, Without Food Stamps, November 14, 2015

Chapter 4: The Church's Call to Care for the Poor

1. Jon Sobrino, The Urgent Need to Return to Being the Church of the Poor, National Catholic Reporter, March 24, 2010

2. Chad Misdiline, 8 Ways Your Church Can Fight Poverty, Churchleaders.com
3. Arloa Sutter, What Your Church Can Do to Care for the Poor, Christianity Today, January 30, 2014
4. Aaron Armstrong, 5 Ways to Help the Poor, Christianity Today, September 2014
5. Lisa Keiser, How Religion Contributes to Wealth, Huffington Post, November 3, 2011
6. Susan Crawford Sullivan, Everyday Religion and Mothers in Poverty, February 2012
7. Susan Crawford Sullivan, Faith and Poverty: Personal Religiosity and Organized Religion in the Lives of Low-Income Urban Mothers, June 5, 2015
8. Rod Dreher, The Church and the Poor: Historical Perspectives, Christian Worldview Journal, March 2, 2012
9. Preston Sprinkle, 4 Ways the Modern Church Looks Nothing Like the Early Church, January 15, 2015
10. Robert D. Lupton, Toxic Charity: How the Church Hurt Those They Help and How to Reverse It, October 11, 2011
11. 1 Thessalonians 4:11, 2 Thessalonians 3:10
12. Deuteronomy 24:17
13. Proverbs 31:6-9
14. Job 29:12
15. 1 John 3:17
16. James 2:15-17
17. Matthew 19:21
18. Luke 4:18
19. Matthew 25:35-40

Chapter 5: Role of Private-Sector Partnerships in Alleviating Poverty

1. Dean Baker, How to Fight Poverty through Full Employment, March 17, 2016

2. Bill Mitchell, The Best Way to Eradicate Poverty Is to Create Jobs, 2011
3. Pamela Roby, S.M. Miller, Education Is the Answer to Poverty, 1970
4. Tim Jacobs, Slavery Legacy: Race-Based Economic Equity, June 2014
5. Andy Medicott, Public-Private Partnerships: Eradicating Poverty through Education, 2011
6. Mona Seragedin, Elda Solloso, and Luis Valenzuela, Local Government Actions to Reduce Poverty and Achieve the Millennium Development Goals, 2014

Chapter 6: Individual and Family Responsibility

1. L. Wenar, Responsibility and Severe Poverty, 2007
2. Charles Murray, In Our Hands: A Plan to Replace the Welfare State, AEI Press, 2006
3. Christopher Winner, et al, Trends in Poverty with an Anchored Supplemental Measure, Columbia Population Research Center, December 2013
4. John Ketchen, Is Personal Responsibility the Means to Ending Poverty?, October 5, 2012
5. Miles Corak, Do Poor Children Become Poor Adults? Discussion Paper, 1993
6. Ruth Lister, From Equality to Social Inclusion: New Labor and the Welfare State, May 1998
7. Robert D. Lupton, Toxic Charity: How the Church Hurt Those They Help and How to Reverse It, October 11, 2011
8. 1 Thessalonians 4:11, 2 Thessalonians 3:10

www.ingramcontent.com/pod-product-compliance
Lightning Source LLC
Chambersburg PA
CBHW071412290526
45789CB00003BA/1251